Bird
Watch

First published 2005
Evans Brothers Limited
2A Portman Mansions
Chiltern Street
London W1U 6NR

British Library Cataloguing in Publication Data

Swallow, Su
        Bird watch. - (Twisters)
        1. Children's stories - Pictorial works
        I. Title
        823.9'14 [J]

ISBN-10: 0237530716
13-digit ISBN (from 1 January 2007) 9780237530716

Printed in China by WKT Company Limited

Series Editor: Nick Turpin
Design: Robert Walster
Production: Jenny Mulvanny
Series Consultant: Gill Matthews

Bird
Watch

Su Swallow
and Simona Dimitri

Evans

"Let's go birdwatching,"
said Dad.

"We need binoculars...

...some lunch...

...and warm clothes."

10

Dad and Ben set off.

They walked a long way.

They sat in a hide...

...and waited.

They ate lunch...

...and listened. No birds.

"Let's go home," said Ben.

24

"No luck?" said Mum.

27

"Birds!"

31

Why not try reading another Twisters book?